Jeffrey Plowman

CAMOUFLAGE & MARKINGS of Axis Armor in the Balkans Campaigns 1940 – 1941

Model Centrum PROGRES

Armor Color Gallery #16

Camouflage & Markings of

Axis Armor in the Balkans Campaigns

1940 – 1941

Jeffrey Plowman

Published by Model Centrum Progres, Poland
Warsaw, March 2019

modelbooks@op.pl

ISBN 978-83-60672-31-0

Edited by **Wojciech J. Gawrych**
Cover layout, design and layout by
PROGRES Publishing House, Warsaw
DTP and prepress by **AIRES-GRAF, Warsaw**
Printed and bound in European Union by
REGIS Ltd., Napoleona 4, 05-230 Kobyłka, Poland

First Edition

Exclusive Distributor
Model Centrum
Warsaw, Poland
wjg-books@wp.pl

Contents

Acknowledgments

I wish to thank the following people for supplying photographs for this book and assisting with information on camouflage: Alain Verwicht, Lee Archer, Bojan Dimitrijević, Wojciech J. Gawrych, Robert Gregory, Péter Kocsis, Péter Mujzer, Dinko Predeović, Larry Te Keoti, Zbigniew Lalak and Shawn Winkler. Other photographs are from my personal archives.

I would also like to thank the following organisations allowing us the use of their photographs: the Bundesarchiv; Fortepan Archive, Budapest; Narodowe Archiwum Cyfrowe [NAC], Warsaw; the Croatian History Museum, Zagreb; ECPAD; the Military Museum, Belgrade; James Payne's "Through Their Eyes" Military Photo Archives for Günther Geucke's image.

Introduction

Despite the tacit agreement between Adolf Hitler, the Chancellor of Germany, and Benito Mussolini, the Prime Minister of Italy, that the Mediterranean was the latter's sphere of influence, Germany had definite designs on the Balkans. This was largely because of their plans to invade and subdue Russia and also because of their fears of British intentions in this region. Hitler saw Britain's interest in Greece as a definite threat, in particular if the British gained control of Crete it would put one of Germany's oil supplies, the Ploesti oilfields in Romania, within range of British bombers. Hitler had also been working hard to recruit other nations in the region to the Tripartite Pact, an agreement between Germany, Italy and Japan that had been signed in September 1940. This led to a series of negotiations between Germany and other states in the Balkans as Hitler pressured them into join the pact. Hungary had already formed a strong alliance with Germany and Italy that enabled them to annex part of Czechoslovakia in 1938 and Subcarpathia the following year. In 1940, Romania was forced to cede Bessarabia and northern Bukovina to Soviet Union. Soon after that Romania came under pressure from Hungary in their push to regain control of other territory. Negotiations between the two countries began in earnest in August, and by the end of the month Romania had agreed to transfer northern Transylvania to Hungary, the handover to be complete two weeks later. This process of annexation continued and on 7 September Romania lost more territory in the south to Bulgaria. Finally on 23 November Romania joined the Axis, German troops moving into the country shortly afterwards.

Though the camouflage employed by German armor in the Balkans was rather bland by comparison with what they used later in the war, they did deploy a wide range of armored vehicles and different styles of tactical markings that varied considerably. However, some of their allies, the Italians and the Hungarians in particular, did have some quite distinctive and interesting camouflage schemes.

Toldi I light tanks from 1 Felderítő Zászlóalj (1st Reconnaissance Battalion), including a command version of the Toldi, pass through a small town in Northern Transylvania in 1940. They are completed in a three-tone scheme of dark olive green overpainted with ochre and red-brown. They carry on their glacis plate and turret sides behind the hatch the Hungarian Maltese-style cross and the white lightning bolt unit insignia on the right mudguard. [Péter Mujzer]

A 35M CV35 tankette emerges from a river in Romania during the Hungarian annexation of Northern Transylvania. It is completed in a three-tone scheme of dark olive green overpainted with ochre and red-brown, and carries the circular Hungarian cross on its lower side plate. Note the official emblem of the Motorised Branch on the upper side plate. [Fortepan]

A Toldi I light command tank (H-313) of 2 Felderítő Zászlóalj (2nd Reconnaissance Battalion) in Transylvania in 1940. It is completed in a three-tone scheme of dark olive green overpainted with ochre and red-brown, with the circular Hungarian cross and the 2F insignia of the unit on the front plate beside the driver's position.

A 39M Csaba armored car and a column of 38M Toldi Is of 1 Felderítő Zászlóalj shortly after entering Piața Petru Maior in Reghin, Northern Transylvania. They are completed in a three-tone scheme of dark olive green overpainted with ochre and red-brown. They carry on their glacis plate and turret sides the Hungarian Maltese-style cross and their lightning strike unit insignia on the right mudguard. The vehicle serial number is in a white rectangle on the right of the front plate, with the Hungarian shield between the letter H and the numbers, the tanks being numbered from front to back: H-322, H-323 and H-321. [Fortepan]

A crowd of people gather round a 39M Csaba armored car from 1 Felderítő Zászlóalj in Piața Petru Maior, Reghin, Northern Transylvania. It is completed in a three-tone scheme of dark olive green overpainted with ochre and red-brown, and carries on its hull roof armor plate and turret sides the early style Hungarian Maltese-style cross plus the white lightning bolt unit insignia on the rear plate. [Péter Mujzer]

39M Csaba armored cars head up a column of Hungarian armor in 1940. They are completed in a three-tone scheme of dark olive green overpainted with ochre and red-brown, and carry the early style Hungarian cross on the turret hull and side, this one a white Maltese-style cross, the arms outlined in red, with a green central boss. [Fortepan]

Crews from 1 Felderítő Zászlóalj rest on their 35M CV33 Tankettes during the annexation of Northern Transylvania in 1940. They are completed in a three-tone scheme of dark olive green overpainted with ochre and red-brown. They carry on their glacis plate sides the Hungarian Maltese-style cross and the white lightning bolt unit insignia on the right mudguard. H-180 also has a skull and crossbones beneath the Hungarian Maltese Cross on its hull side. [Péter Mujzer]

A military policeman directs a 39M Csaba armored car from 2 Felderítő Zászlóalj during the Hungarian annexation of Northern Transylvania. It is completed in a three-tone scheme of dark olive green overpainted with ochre and red-brown, and carries on its glacis plate and hull sides the circular Hungarian cross of a green cross outlined in white, all inside a red circle. It carries its vehicle number above the letters 2FT, the latter indicating that it is 2 Reconnaisance Staff vehicle. [Péter Mujzer]

A column of Toldi I light tanks and 39M Csaba armored cars from 1 Felderítő Zászlóalj halted on the side of the road in Northern Transylvania. They are completed in a three-tone scheme of dark olive green overpainted with ochre and red-brown. They also carry the Hungarian Maltese-style cross on their glacis plates (and turret sides) and their white lightning bolt unit insignia on the right mudguard. [Péter Mujzer]

Farmers reluctantly make way for a 39M Csaba armored car (Pz-166) during the Hungarian annexation of Northern Transylvania in 1940. It is completed in a three-tone scheme of dark olive green overpainted with ochre and red-brown, and carries the circular Hungarian cross on the glacis plate. Between the letters Pz and the number 166 is the red/white/green Hungarian shield. [Fortepan]

The first two 35M CV35 tankettes in this column from the Tankette Company of 2 Felderítő Zászlóalj in Transylvania in 1940 were fitted with Hungarian designed commander's cupolas. They are completed in a three-tone scheme of dark olive green overpainted with ochre and red-brown, and carry the circular Hungarian cross on their glacis and side plates and their unit insignia 2F on the front plate. [Péter Mujzer]

35M CV35 tankettes from 14 Bicycle Battalion during the advance into Transylvania in 1940. They are completed in a three-tone scheme of dark olive green overpainted with ochre and red-brown and carry their platoon insignia on the superstructure side of a white skull with dagger. The rear vehicle has the identification number 163. [Péter Mujzer]

The crew of this 39M Csaba armored car (Pz-134) have stopped for a break during the Hungarian drive into Northern Transylvania in 1940. The vehicle is completed in a three-tone scheme of dark olive green overpainted with ochre and red-brown, and carries the circular Hungarian cross on the glacis plate. [Fortepan]

A Toldi I light tank (H-344) of 1 Lovas Páncélos Zászlóalj (1st Armored Cavalry Battalion) during the Hungarian occupation of Transylvania in 1940. It is completed in a three-tone scheme of dark olive green overpainted with ochre and red-brown, and carries its unit's horse insignia and the Motorized Branch insignia on its turret. [Péter Mujzer]

A column of 39M Csaba armored cars from 2 Felderítő Zászlóalj line a street in Northern Transylvania during its occupation by Hungarian troops. They are completed in a three-tone scheme of dark olive green overpainted with ochre and red-brown, and carry circular Hungarian crosses with the unit insignia 2F on the tool locker on right mudguard. [Péter Mujzer]

War in Albanian Epirus

The dispute between Greece and Italy can be traced back to the end of the Balkan Wars in 1913 with the creation of Albania, when the Greeks within it set up the Autonomous Republic of Epirus. This Greece occupied at the start of the First World War, until driven out by the Italians in 1917. Then in April 1939, following Germany's annexation of Austria, Italy sent troops into Albania, occupying its capital, Tirana, and forcing the Albanian king to flee to Greece. After their abortive attack on France in 1940 Mussolini turned his attention to Yugoslavia and Greece, until Hitler dissuaded him from following this course of action. Instead he launched an attack on the British forces in Egypt, the Italian army under Marshall Radolfo Graziani reaching as far as Mersa Matruh before running out of steam. However, following the occupation of Romania by Germany in October, Mussolini set about planning an invasion of Greece.

Thus in the early hours of the morning of 28 October 1940 the Italians sent an ultimatum to the Greek government demanding that they be allowed to occupy parts of Greece. When this was refused by the Greek Prime Minister, General Ioannis Metaxas, Italian forces crossed the frontier in Epirus. Caught by surprise the Greeks were initially forced to give ground along the Elaia–Kalamas River Line as 51 Divisione di Fanteria "Siena" and 23 Divisione "Ferrara", backed up by the 131 Divisione Corazzata "Centauro", thrust towards Elaia. However, the marshy terrain over which the attack was conducted proved too much for the "Centauro's" tanks and the attack soon ground to a halt. The Italians had more success on their right flank, securing a bridgehead over the Kalamas River in November, while their 3 Divisione Alpina "Julia" captured the village of Vovousa but was unable to secure the Metsovo Pass. Then in mid-November the Greeks counter-attacked and within a week had re-crossed the Kalamas River before taking the war into Albania, securing its only other port in the south and taking Klissoura in the centre before wintry blizzards and storms brought their offensive an end.

An Italian soldier and some Albanian civilians inspect an M13/40 from 4th Medium Tank Battalion, 131 Divisione Corazzato "Centauro". The tank is completed in overall dark grey-green, with the white Roman numeral IV beneath the company rectangle insignia on the hull door.

A L3/33 tankette being unloaded from a transport ship at the port of Durrës, Albania in April 1939. Though not evident in this photograph it would be completed in their pre-war scheme of red-brown overpainted with dark-grey-green blotches. The two vertical stripes on the side indicates the tankette is from the 2nd Platoon of its company. [Zbigniew Lalak]

L3/33 tankettes disembarking from the seaplane tender "Giuseppe Miraglia" at Durrës, Albania on 12 April 1939. They would be completed in their pre-war scheme of red-brown overpainted with dark grey-green blotches. [NAC]

An M13/40 tank from 4th Medium Tank Battalion, 131 Divisione Corazzato "Centauro" in Albania in 1940. It is completed in a scheme of dark grey-green overall. It also carries the company insignia on the hull side door and beneath it the Roman letter IV.

A L3/35Lf (Lanciaflamme) operating in the mountains of Albania in 1940. It is completed in a two-tone scheme of red-brown overpainted with dark grey-green blotches, while the vertical stripes indicates that this might be from the 1st Platoon of its company.

These M13/40 crews from 4th Medium Tank Battalion, 131 Divisione Corazzato "Centauro" in Albania in 1940, have added foliage in an attempt to further camouflage their tanks. Note the licence plate R^{O}E^{TO} 2832 on the rear of the right hand tank.

First Lieutenant Galli's wrecked M13/40 from the 3rd Platoon, 2nd Company, 4th Medium Tank Battalion, 131 Divisione Corazzato "Centauro" at Monastir Hill, March 1941. It is completed in overall dark grey-green, with three vertical stripes indicating it was from the 3rd Platoon of the 1st Company. Below this insignia is the Roman letter IV indicating this tank is from the 4th Medium Tank Battalion. To the left of the driver's visor is a playing card insignia of seven red diamonds on a white rectangle. This was a platoon identification marking used only in the Balkans. [Daniele Guglielmi]

Bulgaria joins the Axis

Critical to German plans in the Balkans was the need to involve Bulgaria. At the outbreak of W.W.II Bulgaria had declared their neutrality but, with the Italian attack on Epirus and Greece having failed, the Bulgarian government found themselves coming under increased pressure to join the Tripartite Pact and permit the passage of German forces through their country. On the surface this was to allow Germany to attack Greece, though the real reason was to secure their southern flank prior to their invasion of Russia. At this stage, however, Germany only intended to take over the northern Aegean littoral region of Greece. To achieve this Germany also needed free passage of their troops through Hungary, something they obtained at the end of November 1940 when Hungary joined the Tripartite Pact, telling the Hungarians that this was only because they wanted to provide support to the Italians.

Towards the end of December 1940 the Germans started to build up their Luftwaffe units in Romania, in particular their army cooperation units. In the last week of that month the first units intended for Greece began passing through Hungary. Among them was the heavy pontoon bridging equipment needed to cross the Danube River. Work on this bridge, to be sited between Giurgui, Romania to Ruse, Bulgaria, was supposed to start at the beginning of January 1941 but heavy snows forced them to put off this for another month. At this stage the Bulgarians were offering free passage of German units through their country but were still refusing to join the Axis. However, on 1 March 1941 this changed with the Bulgarian government signing of the Tripartite Pact and four days later the first German troops rolled across the Danube River.

A PzKpfw III Ausf. G from 9. Panzer-Division leads a column of armor, including two Kleiner Panzerbefehlswagens, across the German pontoon bridge over the Danube between Romania and Bulgaria on 5 March 1941. It is completed in overall Dunkelgrau, with the divisional insignia on the front plate to the left of the driver's visor.

A PzKpfw IV Ausf. D leads a column of other PzKpfw IVs from 9. Panzer-Division over the Danube to Bulgaria from Romania on 5 March 1941. The lead vehicle is completed in overall Dunkelgrau, with the divisional insignia on the front plate to the left of the driver's visor.

PzKpfw IIIs from 9. Panzer-Division passing through a small village in Bulgaria. They are completed in overall Dunkelgrau. The rear vehicle, possibly a PzKpfw III Ausf. G, carries its vehicle number 201 on a plate on the rear stowage rack, while below it on the rear hull is the number 2 next to a tank company symbol. [NAC]

Photographed on 7 March 1941, these two PzKpfw III Ausf. Gs in a rural part of Bulgaria appear to be in the process of being resupplied. Both tanks are completed in overall Dunkelgrau.

PzKpfw I Ausf. B tanks from 9. Panzer-Division crossing the Danube between Romania and Bulgaria on 5 March 1941. They are completed in overall Dunkelgrau.

The Germans had to construct more temporary bridges as they moved through Bulgaria, such as the one this SdKfz 251/3 Ausf. B is crossing. Completed in overall Dunkelgrau it has Balkenkreuz between the driver's and spare driver's visors. The other markings appear to have been erased by the wartime censor.

On 11 March 1941 this crowd of Bulgarian women gathered to talk to the crew of this PzKpfw III Ausf. E Befehlswagen. That it is still in transit is evident by the turret rack of jerricans and the extra jerricans on the trackguard. It is completed in overall Dunkelgrau.

Mixed up in this column of tanks from 9. Panzer-Division in the process of passing through a small Bulgarian village is a PzKpfw III Ausf. G and a deturreted PzKpfw I converted to use as a munitions carrier. Both tanks are completed in overall Dunkelgrau, with the divisional insignia on the front plate to the right of the driver's visor on the PzKpfw III.

A column of PzKpfw III tanks from 2. Panzer-Division passing through Sofia, Bulgaria on 9 March 1941. The lead tank is an Ausf. G and that behind an Ausf. H, with additional frontal armor. They are completed in overall Dunkelgrau, with the divisional insignia on the front plate to the right of the driver's visor. The lead tank carries its vehicle number 415 on the hull side plate, and a square on the turret side.

A PzKpfw III Ausf. H from 2. Panzer-Division in Sofia, Bulgaria on 9 March 1941, note the additional bolt on armor on the hull. It is completed in overall Dunkelgrau, with the divisional insignia on the front plate to the right of the driver's visor.

The crew of a StuG III Ausf. B of Sturmgeschütz-Abteilung 191 during a break in their advance through Bulgaria in 1941. The vehicle is completed overall in Dunkelgrau, it carries the unit insignia of a red bull in a black rectangle, the latter outlined in red on its front mudguard, while it carries a Balkenkreuz on the superstructure side. [Plowman Collection]

Personnel from Sturmgeschütz-Abteilung 191 gather round a StuG III Ausf. B presumably for an address from their commanding officer. Completed in overall Dunkelgrau it carries the Balkenkreuz on the superstructure side plate. [Bundesarchiv]

A Schwerer Panzerspähwagen SdKfz 231 8-rad (WH-296428) leads a column through a mountain pass in Bulgaria. Completed in overall Dunkelgrau the armored car lacks a visible divisional insignia but has the number 191 under the reconnaissance company symbol on its left mudguard suggesting it might be from Sturmgeschütz-Abteilung 191. [Bundesarchiv]

Bulgarians gather round a Leichter Gepanzerter Beobachtungskraftwagen SdKfz 253 from Sturmgeschütz-Abteilung 191. Completed in overall Dunkelgrau, it carries the unit insignia of a red bull in a black rectangle, the latter outlined in red. The symbol on the left side of the front plate is that of an assault gun battery, while the symbol on the plate between the visors suggests it was from 2. Kompanie. It has a Balkenkreuz on the upper side armor. [Bundesarchiv]

The attack on Yugoslavia

Yugoslavia had come under pressure from both Britain and Germany to join them in an alliance early on in the war. The first German overtures were made on 14 February 1941 and were followed by further meetings on 4 March at which time Hitler offered them access to the sea via Salonika and made the promise that Yugoslavia would not be required to permit the passage of German troops over its soil. The Yugoslavs finally succumbed to German pressure four weeks later and signed their Tripartite Pact but it was to be short lived. On the night of 26/27 March the Yugoslav military seized power in a coup d'état. Despite the assurances from the new Yugoslav government, that they wanted to maintain their friendly status, Hitler was determined to seize control of the country by military means and so set in motion plans to do so.

Thus on the morning of 6 April the Luftwaffe appeared in force over Belgrade, the capital of Yugoslavia, and subjected the city to a severe pounding that continued for the next two days, one consequence of this being that it cut all communication between the Yugoslav high command and its armies in the field. Their air force was all but wiped out as well. Though the main attack was not supposed to start until 10 April, some German units proceeded to secure bridge along the border with Yugoslavia. Emboldened by this success, they carried on further south into the country, causing Croatian units to mutiny, while the bulk of the Yugoslav army pulled back to Zagreb. Thus by the time the bulk of German invasion forces crossed the border their progress through Croatia was relatively unimpeded by the Yugoslav army and they were able to enter Zagreb later that afternoon. Two days later, after the Luftwaffe bombing of Ljubljana, the Italians moved into Yugoslavia, linking up with 14. Panzer-Division on the road between Rijeka and Karlovac.

German forces also crossed the border in the south on 8 April, initially meeting little resistance in their drive towards Belgrade. However, Belgrade itself was secured by a small force of SS troops from Das Reich who entered the city late one afternoon and seized control. This taken, the German forces swung to the south towards Sarajevo, in a two-pronged drive, the aim being to cut off the escape of Yugoslav troops to Greece. On 15 April both arms of this drive closed on the city and two day's later the Yugoslav army capitulated.

Hungary also used the German invasion as an excuse to protect Hungarians in the now dismembered Yugoslavia by crossing the border and striking south towards the Danube river between the confluence of the Vukovar and Tisza rivers. As the Yugoslav resistance had all but collapsed by now they did so without encountering significant resistance.

The crew of a PzKpfw III Ausf. H Befehlswagen pass a line of horse-drawn supply wagons in Yugoslavia. It is completed in overall Dunkelgrau. [Dinko Predoević]

14. Panzer-Division

A Leichter Panzerspähwagen (MG) SdKfz 221 from 14. Panzer-Division is greeted by enthusiastic Croatians as it enters Ban Josip Jelačić Square in Zagreb on 11 April. It is completed in overall Dunkelgrau. [Croatian History Museum via Bojan Dimitrijević]

A Schwerer Panzerspähwagen SdKfz 231 8-rad from 14. Panzer-Division wends its way through the crowd in Ban Josip Jelačić Square in Zagreb on 11 April. It is completed in overall Dunkelgrau and carries the tactical symbol of a reconnaissance company on its glacis plate. [Croatian History Museum via Bojan Dimitrijević]

A Schwerer Panzerfunkwagen SdKfz 263 8-rad from 14. Panzer-Division among the crowds in Ban Josip Jelačić Square in Zagreb on 11 April. It is completed in overall Dunkelgrau and carries the tactical symbol of a reconnaissance company on its glacis plate. [Croatian History Museum via Bojan Dimitrijević]

A PzKpfw II Ausf. C from the light platoon of 1. Kompanie, 14. Panzer-Division making a circuit around Ban Josip Jelačić Square in Zagreb on 11 April. It is completed in overall Dunkelgrau, with the divisional insignia to the right side of the driver's visor and a vehicle identification of IL2 on the turret side. [Croatian History Museum via Bojan Dimitrijević]

A PzKpfw II Ausf. C from the light platoon of 8. Kompanie, 14. Panzer-Division proceeding along Ilica Street in Zagreb on 11 April. It is completed in overall Dunkelgrau, with a vehicle identification of 8L5 on the turret side. [Croatian History Museum via Bojan Dimitrijević]

PzKpfw II Ausf. Cs of the light platoon of 5. Kompanie, 14. Panzer-Division line a street in Zagreb on 11 April. They are completed in overall Dunkelgrau, with the divisional insignia on the left side of the driver's visor, the Balkenkreuz on the hull side and vehicle identification numbers on the turret side. From left to right these are 5L5, 5L4, 5L3 and 5L2. [Croatian History Museum via Dinko Predoević]

Later this column of tanks was photographed just inside Ban Josip Jelačić Square in Zagreb on 11 April. The PzKpfw II Ausf. C, fitted with additional armor plates bolted to the turret front and hull front, is completed in overall Dunkelgrau and carries the Balkenkreuz on the hull side. Its vehicle identification, on the turret side, appears to be 5L5, indicating it is from the light platoon of 5. Kompanie. [Croatian History Museum via Dinko Predoević]

Behind the PzKpfw II Ausf. C was this Pzkpfw III Ausf. H. It is completed in overall Dunkelgrau and carries the divisional insignia between the driver's visor and the hull machine gun mount. [Croatian History Museum via Dinko Predoević]

PzKpfw IIIs from 14. Panzer-Division line a street in Zagreb on 11 April, an Ausf. F on the left, an Ausf. G Befehlswagen and possibly an Ausf. G on the right. They are completed in overall Dunkelgrau, the tank in the centre having divisional insignia between the driver's visor and pistol port. [Croatian History Museum via Bojan Dimitrijević]

A PzKpfw III Ausf. H from 14. Panzer-Division parked in Ban Josip Jelačić Square in Zagreb on 11 April. It is completed in overall Dunkelgrau, with a Balkenkreuz on a box holding spare jerricans, that partly obscure its turret numbers. [Croatian History Museum via Dinko Predoević]

Two PzKpfw III Ausf. Hs from 14. Panzer-Division line a street in Zagreb on 11 April. They are completed in overall Dunkelgrau, with their divisional insignia between the driver's visor and hull gun mount. Their turret numbers are partly obscured by the stowage of extra jerricans on the track guard. [Croatian History Museum via Dinko Predoević]

PzKpfw III Ausf. Gs from 14. Panzer-Division line a street in Zagreb on 11 April. They are completed in overall Dunkelgrau and the one on the left appears to have the identification number 441. [Croatian History Museum via Bojan Dimitrijević]

PzKpfw IIIs from 14. Panzer-Division line a street in Zagreb on 11 April, an Ausf. E in front and two Ausf. Gs beyond it. They are completed in overall Dunkelgrau. [Croatian History Museum via Bojan Dimitrijević]

A platoon of PzKpfw III from 3 Zug, 5 Kompanie, 14. Panzer-Division line a street in Zagreb on 11 April. The second from left appears to be an Ausf. F, the rest are Ausf. Gs. They are completed in overall Dunkelgrau, one with a Balkenkreuz on the hull side. Their turret numbers, from left to right, are: 534, 533, 532 and 531. [Croatian History Museum via Dinko Predoević]

A PzKpfw III Ausf. G Befehlswagen from 14. Panzer-Division in the rain in Zagreb on 11 April. It is completed in overall Dunkelgrau, with a Balkenkreuz on the hull side and the divisional insignia forward of the visor on the turret. [Croatian History Museum via Dinko Predoević]

The crew of this PzKpfw IV Ausf. D from 14. Panzer-Division take advantage of the break in Zagreb on 11 April to clean the barrel of their 75 mm KwK 37 L/24. It is completed in overall Dunkelgrau and carries the Balkenkreuz on the hull side. Part of its identification number on the turret 4 can also been seen suggesting it was from 4. Kompanie. [Croatian History Museum via Dinko Predoević]

Croatians inspect a PzKpfw IV Ausf. D or E from 4. Zug, 4. Kompanie, 14. Panzer-Division in Karlovac on 11 or 12 April. It is completed in overall Dunkelgrau, with Balkenkreuz on its hull side. Its turret number is 445. [Dinko Predoević]

Yugoslav soldiers talk to the crew of this PzKpfw II Ausf. C from 4. Kompanie, 14. Panzer-Division in Niš on 15 April. Completed in overall Dunkelgrau, it carries the divisional insignia on the turret rear along with its vehicle identification number 4L6.

Croatians gather beside the Sava River to watch the crossing of armor from 14. Panzer-Division. Among the tanks was this PzKpfw III Ausf. G. It is completed in overall Dunkelgrau. [Larry Te Keoti]

After taking part in the campaign 14. Panzer-Division was withdrawn from Yugoslavia, crossing over the Sava River to Slavonski Brod by ferry, this PzKpfw IV Ausf. D among them. It is completed in overall Dunkelgrau. [Larry Te Keoti]

[Above right] Among the tanks from 14. Panzer-Division transported over the Sava River to Slavonski Brod was this PzKpfw III als Tauchpanzer based on the Ausf. H. It is completed in overall Dunkelgrau. [Larry Te Keoti]

Another of the tanks from 14. Panzer-Division unloaded at Slavonski Brod was this PzKpfw III Ausf. H. It is completed in overall Dunkelgrau. [Dinko Predoević]

11. Panzer-Division

A PzKpfw III Ausf. G Befehlswagen from 11. Panzer-Division passing by a small village in Yugoslavia. It is completed in overall Dunkelgrau, with a Balkenkreuz on the hull side and the Ghost Rider divisional insignia on the right side of the pistol port. In addition to these there is a rampant horse between the pistol port and the driver's visor. Markings on the turret include: vehicle number 01, a colored circle and what looks like another version of the division's ghost insignia. [Alain Verwicht]

A column of armor from 11. Panzer-Division on the move along a muddy road in Yugoslavia. All vehicles are completed in overall Dunkelgrau. The second vehicle in line, a Schützenpanzerwagen SdKfz 251/1 Ausf. B, has the symbol of a motorized infantry platoon below its divisional insignia. The Kleiner Panzerbefehlswagen behind it has the number 03 above the driver's visor. [ECPAD via Alain Verwicht]

A PzKpfw III from 11. Panzer-Division following the route of a railway in Yugoslavia. It is completed in overall Dunkelgrau, with the divisional insignia next to the Balkenkreuz on the hull rear, while another Balkenkreuz can be seen on the side. [Bundesarchiv via Alain Verwicht)

A column of PzKpfw IV tanks from 11. Panzer-Division, led by an Ausf. E, pass the 54 kilometer mark on a road in Croatia. They are completed in overall Dunkelgrau, with the divisional insignia between the driver's visor and the hull machine gun on the lead tank. [Dinko Predoević]

The crew of this PzKpfw IV Ausf. E from 11. Panzer-Division take a break during the drive through Yugoslavia. The tank is completed in overall Dunkelgrau, with the divisional insignia in between driver's visor and the hull machine gun mount. The divisional insignia also appears in front of the driver's side visor, followed by the Division's ghost insignia, further back beside the unit's Balkenkreuz on the hull side. It also carries its vehicle identification number 11 below the visor on the turret side. [Bundesarchiv]

A column of PzKpfw II Ausf. Cs from 11. Panzer-Division negotiate a muddy road in Yugoslavia. Completed in overall Dunkelgrau the lead vehicle carries the Balkenkreuz and ghost insignia of the division on the hull side and the identification number 42 above two lozenge-shaped markings on the turret. [Bundesarchiv via Alain Verwicht]

An umbrella comes in handy for the commander of this Kleiner Panzerbefehlswagen command tank from 11. Panzer-Division in the rain in Yugoslavia. Though its overall Dunkelgrau is streaked in mud the divisional insignia is still visible beneath the machine gun mount. [ECPAD via Alain Verwicht]

[Far right] A PzKpfw III Ausf. G from 11. Panzer-Division on the road to Banja Luka on 13 April 1941. It is completed in overall Dunkelgrau. [Dinko Predoević]

A PzKpfw III Ausf. E from 11. Panzer-Division on the road to Banja Luka on 13 April 1941. It is completed in overall Dunkelgrau and carries the divisional insignia on the hull side, along with its vehicle number 22 on the turret. [Dinko Predoević]

[Below] A PzKpfw III Ausf. E from 11. Panzer-Division in Yugoslavia. It is completed in overall Dunkelgrau, with the divisional insignia on the hull front between the driver's visor and hull machine gun and this insignia, the Division's ghost insignia and Balkenkreuz on the hull side. It carries its vehicle number 35 on the turret. [Zbigniew Lalak]

[Below right] A PzKpfw IV Ausf. E from 11. Panzer-Division on the road to Banja Luka on 13 April 1941. It is completed in overall Dunkelgrau, has a Balkenkreuz on the hull and its vehicle number 21 on the turret. [Dinko Predoević]

184. Sturmgeschütz-Abteilung

A column of StuG III Ausf. Bs from 184. Sturmgeschütz-Abteilung in Yugoslavia waiting for their movement orders. They are completed in overall Dunkelgrau and carry the Balkenkreuz as well as their vehicle identification number on the side, the latter being repeated on the hull rear. From left to right these numbers are: 34, 32 and 22. [Dinko Predoević]

A StuG III Ausf. B crew taking a break while other artillery roll past them. It is completed in overall Dunkelgrau and carries the number 34 on the rear plate suggesting it is from 3. Batterie of 184. Stug-Abteilung. [Dinko Predoević]

The crew of this StuG III Ausf. B appear to be refueling their vehicle. It is completed in overall Dunkelgrau and carries the letter F on the rear plate. [Dinko Predoević]

[Bottom] The entry of 184. Sturmgeschütz-Abteilung into Yugoslavia appeared to be of considerable interest to the locals. These two StuG III Ausf. Bs are completed in overall Dunkelgrau and carry the Balkenkreuz on the side as well as their vehicle identification numbers, 22 in front and 24 behind, suggesting these are from 2. Batterie. [Dinko Predoević]

[Right] Two Leichter Gepanzereter Beobachtungskraftwagen SdKfz 253s in Yugoslavia. They are both completed in overall Dunkelgrau, vehicle number 31 (licence plate WH-685592) has its Balkenkreuz on the hull side as well as its vehicle identification number. Both it and WH-685591 carry the tactical symbol of an assault gun battery. [Dinko Predoević]

[Below right] Crews rest on their Leichter Gepanzereter Beobachtungskraftwagen SdKfz 253s in Yugoslavia. They are all completed in overall Dunkelgrau, with a Balkenkreuz on the hull side as well as their vehicle identification number on the hull side and rear. Number 31 is in the foreground, while behind it are 21 (licence plate WH-685591) and 11. [Dinko Predoević]

31
WH-685 597
WH-685 591

21
11
31

133 Divisione Corazzato "Littorio"

An M13/40 from 133 Divisione Corazzato "Littorio" in Rijeka on 11 April. It is completed in a scheme of dark grey-green overall. [Dinko Predoević]

An L3/33 tankette from 133 Divisione Corazzato "Littorio" being carried through Rijeka on its special trailer on 11 April. It is completed in red-brown overpainted with dark grey-green blotches. The three vertical stripes indicates it is from the 3rd Platoon of its company. [Dinko Predoević]

A column of L3/35Lf (Lanciaflamme) tankettes from 133 Divisione Corazzato "Littorio" driving through Rijeka on 11 April. They would all be completed in red-brown overpainted with dark grey-green blotches. The rear L3/35Lf has the numbers 33 and 1 on the rear plate of the superstructure. [Dinko Predoević]

Hungarian Armor

A Toldi I light tank passes a column of mounted troops during the Hungarian invasion of Yugoslavia in 1941. It is completed in a three-tone scheme of dark olive green overpainted with ochre and red-brown, and carries the octagonal Hungarian cross on its glacis plate and turret side doors. [Péter Mujzer]

A 38M Toldi I light tank (H-366) passing through Villány, Hungary in April 1941 on its way to Yugoslavia. It is completed in a three-tone scheme of dark olive green overpainted with ochre and red-brown, and carries the circular Hungarian cross on its glacis plate and turret sides. Just visible on the turret is the official emblem of the Motorized Branch. The vehicle serial number H-366 is inside a white rectangle on the right hand side of the front plate. [Fortepan]

[This page] A column of 38M Toldi I light tanks on the road in Yugoslavia in 1941. They are completed in a three-tone scheme of dark olive green overpainted with ochre and red-brown, and carry the octagonal Hungarian cross on their glacis plates and turret sides. The tank in the bottom photo has the vehicle serial number H-356 inside a white rectangle on the right hand side of the front plate. [Fortepan]

A Toldi I light tank (H-303) of 2 Felderítő Zászlóalj in Yugoslavia in 1941. It is completed in a three-tone scheme of dark olive green overpainted with ochre and red-brown and carries the octagonal Hungarian cross on its glacis plate and the tank insignia of the unit on the front plate beside the driver's position. [Péter Mujzer]

This Toldi I light tank motors through Vukovar in northern Croatia during the Hungarian invasion of Yugoslavia in 1941. It is completed in a three-tone scheme of dark olive green overpainted with ochre and red-brown, and, though not visible would have had its Hungarian identification markings on the glacis plate and side doors of the turret. [Péter Mujzer]

The crew of a Toldi I light tank taking a break in Yugoslavia in 1941. It is completed in a three-tone scheme of dark olive green overpainted with ochre and red-brown, and carries the octagonal Hungarian cross on its turret sides along with the official emblem of the Motorized Branch. [Péter Mujzer]

A column of Toldi I light tanks of 1 Lovas Páncélos Zászlóalj (1st Armored Cavalry Battalion) during the Hungarian invasion of Yugoslavia in 1941. The lead tank (H-392) is completed in a three-tone scheme of dark olive green overpainted with ochre and red-brown and carries the octagonal Hungarian cross. At least two tanks have the white Turul bird insignia on their turret hatch, which was the Light Tank Company sign. [Péter Mujzer]

[Far right] A column of 35M CV35 tankettes during the Hungarian invasion of Yugoslavia in April 1941. They are completed in a three-tone scheme of dark olive green overpainted with ochre and red-brown. [Péter Mujzer]

These Toldi I light tanks make their way gingerly past a column horse-drawn wagons during the Hungarian entry into Yugoslavia in 1941. The lead tank (H-392) is completed in a three-tone scheme of dark olive green overpainted with ochre and red-brown. The crew appear to have tried to mask the Hungarian cross on the glacis plate. [Péter Mujzer]

This 39M Csaba armored car from 1 Felderítő Zászlóalj appears to have run onto a mine in Serbia during their invasion of Yugoslavia in 1941. It is completed in a three-tone scheme of dark olive green overpainted with ochre and red-brown, and carries the white Maltese-style Hungarian cross on the hull side and glacis plates. [Fortepan]

A column of 39M Csaba armored cars from 1 Felderítő Zászlóalj waiting for the roads to be opened up during the Hungarian invasion of Yugoslavia in 1941. Pc-158 was completed in a three-tone scheme of dark olive green overpainted with ochre and red-brown, and carries the white Maltese-style Hungarian cross on the turret hull and side and glacis plate, and its white lightning bolt insignia on the glacis plate. [Péter Mujzer]

Other armored units

The Germans also pressed the French UE tractor into service as the UE 630(f). This one in Bosnia, completed in overall Dunkelgrau, has the lettering IV on the front and locker on the side. [Dinko Predoević]

A column of heavily loaded down tanks proceeds through a Bosnian town. The rear tank, a PzKpfw III Ausf. G or H, carries its identification number 622 on the turret rear. All are completed in overall Dunkelgrau. [Dinko Predoević]

A UE 630(f) in service with the Germans in Bosnia. It is completed in overall Dunkelgrau. [Dinko Predoević]

German officers addressing soldiers from a PzKpfw IV Ausf. B somewhere in Bosnia, possibly after the cessation of hostilities. The tank is completed in overall Dunkelgrau with a Balkenkreuz on its hull side. [Dinko Predoević]

A StuG III Ausf. B from 191. Sturmgeschütz-Abteilung in Belgrade in April 1941. Completed in overall Dunkelgrau, it carries the unit insignia of a red bull in a black rectangle, the latter outlined in red, on the right mudguard. [Military Museum, Belgrade via Bojan Dimitrijević]

A Leichter Panzerspähwagen (2 cm) SdKfz 222 passing the saluting stand in Sarajevo, Bosnia on 22 April 1941. It is completed in overall Dunkelgrau with a large Balkenkreuz over the radiator.

A StuG III in Belgrade after the invasion. It is completed in overall Dunkelgrau and has a Balkankreuz on the hull side. Also in evidence is a white square on a locker on the side. [NAC]

The invasion of Greece

The British response to the Italian invasion of Epirus led to their sending troops to Crete, a move that angered Germany, because they felt that Italy should have occupied Crete first. Though the Greeks were anxious to keep Britain out of the war, the British did send over some air force units. This prompted the Germans to revise their plans for the invasion of Greece to a full occupation, timed to take place around the same time as their occupation of Yugoslavia. The British in the meantime finally managed to convince the Greeks to accept an expeditionary force of an armored brigade and three infantry divisions, though only two of the latter were actually sent.

The Germans eventually launched their attack on 6 April 1941. In the east, while their mountain troops launched a direct assault on the Metaxas Line, an armored force swung around behind this position and onto Salonika, capturing it three days later. That same day in the west the Germans ran up against the British and Commonwealth defences at Kliedi Pass. Set up to block the Germans until another defensive line could be established further south, these troops managing to hold out against the German assault until 13 April.

Two days later the German attack then fell on ANZAC troops at Servia and Olympus Passes and at Platamon on the east coast. Though the line was easily held at Servia and Olympus, the battalion sent to hold Platamon was forced to fall back to Pineios Gorge when a strong armored thrust threatened to unhinge the entire defensive line. By this stage plans were well in advance to withdraw to the next defensive line at Thermopylae so the troops at Pineios were reinforced by two more battalions of infantry and some artillery, while the withdrawal of the rest of expeditionary force stepped up and escaped the trap. Back at Thermopylae the decision was made to evacuate the British expeditionary force from Greece, so a delaying action was held here while plans for the evacuation were stepped up. In the end the bulk of the British and Commonwealth force was successfully withdrawn, many of the troops being offloaded on Crete.

Moving along the railway line below Platamon Ridge, I/3. Panzer-Regiment, 2. Panzer-Division found progress was slow, at least one tank has come to grief and requires a tow. The PzKpfw III Ausf. G tank beside the track and the PzKpfw III Ausf. H in front both appear to have the Balkenkreuz on their turret sides. [Bundesarchiv]

2. Panzer-Division

An early model PzKpfw III Ausf. G with a 37 mm gun, up-armored to Ausf. H standard, from 3. Panzer-Regiment passing the Hamza Bey mosque in Salonika on 9 April 1941. It is completed in overall Dunkelgrau and carries its divisional insignia on the front plate to the right of the driver's visor. [Bundesarchiv]

A column of PzKpfw III tanks from 3. Panzer-Regiment passing through Salonika on 9 April 1941. The lead tank appears to be an Ausf. H. It, like the others, is completed in overall Dunkelgrau, with a Balkenkreuz on the hull side. The divisional insignia on the front plate on the left side of the driver's visor appears to have been obscured by the censor. Perhaps one of the best known images from the Greek campaign, this photograph has been "flaked" (presumably by the Germans) by the addition, in the foreground, of two men offering Nazi-style salutes to the column of tanks.

A PzKpfw IV Ausf. D from 3. Panzer-Regiment in Salonika on 9 April. It is completed in overall Dunkelgrau, with the divisional insignia on the front plate to the right of the driver's visor.

A SdKfz 251/6 mittlerer Kommander-Panzerwagen Ausf. A (WH-645249) from 3. Panzer-Regiment in Salonika on 9 April. It is completed in overall Dunkelgrau and carries the symbol for an infantry signal platoon on its left mudguard. [Bundesarchiv]

A SdKfz 251/6 mittlerer Kommander-Panzerwagen Ausf. A (WH-645249) from 2. Panzer-Division on the waterfront at Salonika on 9 April. It is completed in overall Dunkelgrau and carries the symbol for an infantry signal platoon on its left mudguard. [Bundesarchiv]

A PzKpfw III moving through some rough ground in Greece. The style of its vehicle identification number, 215, suggests that it might be from 2. Panzer-Division. It is completed in overall Dunkelgrau. Note how it is using the swastika flag over the engine deck as an air recognition symbol. [Bundesarchiv via Alain Verwicht]

A PzKpfw III Ausf. F from 2. Zug, 1. Kompanie, I/3. Panzer-Regiment near Platamon on 17 April. It is completed in overall Dunkelgrau, while it carries on its side plate the divisional insignia (above which is the number 61016), the tactical symbol of tank company with number 2 beside it, a Balkenkreuz and its identification number 123. On the turret it carries a spade playing card symbol. [Bundesarchiv]

The crew of this PzKpfw III (possibly an Ausf. E, F or G) from 2. Zug, 2. Kompanie, I/3. Panzer-Regiment appear to have stopped to talk to some local Greeks. Completed in overall Dungelgrau it has a horseshoe marking on the turret. On the hull it carries the tactical symbol of tank company with number 2, its identification number 225 on a lozenge-shaped plate on the side and a Balkenkreuz.

A column of tanks from I/3. Panzer-Regiment advancing on the railway line below Platamon Ridge on 17 April 1941. The lead tank appears to be PzKpfw III Ausf. G, while behind it is an Ausf. H. [Bundesarchiv]

Tanks from I/3. Panzer-Regiment after their descent from the Platamon Ridge on 17 April 1941. The lead tank appears to be PzKpfw III Ausf. F, while behind it is a PzKpfw IV Ausf. D. [Bundesarchiv]

PzKpfw III Ausf. G leads a column of tanks from I/3. Panzer-Regiment along the railway line in Pineios Gorge on 18 April. It is completed in overall Dunkelgrau, with its divisional insignia to the right of the driver's visor. [Bundesarchiv]

A heavily loaded down Krankenpanzerwagen SdKfz 251/8 (WH-609058) from 3. Panzer-Regiment approaching the first tunnel along the railway line in Pineios Gorge on 18 April 1941. It is completed in overall Dunkelgrau and carries its Balkenkreuz on the upper part of the rear door. Its divisional insignia is on the lower part of the rear door, below the tactical symbol of tank company and the letter R indicating it is from Regimental Headquarters. [Bundesarchiv]

PzKpfw II Ausf. Cs from 3. Panzer-Regiment passing through Larissa on 19 April. The second tank in line is completed in overall Dunkelgrau with a Balkenkreuz on the hull side, it also appears to have triangle on its turret.

A PzKpfw III Ausf. G tank from I/3. Panzer-Regiment working its way up the Pineios River on 18 April. It is completed in overall Dunkelgrau, with its divisional insignia on the upper left corner of the front plate and the number 65948 on the front corner of the side plate. It also appears to have a diamond insignia on the turret. [Bundesarchiv]

A PzKpfw III from I/3. Panzer-Regiment with troops on board about to enter the water in Pineios Gorge on 18 April. Its 37 mm gun suggests that it was either an Ausf. E or F. It is completed in overall Dunkelgrau. [Bundesarchiv]

PzKpfw III Ausf. F from II/3. Panzer-Regiment on its way through Larissa on 19 April. It is completed in overall Dunkelgrau, with a Balkenkreuz on the hull side and what appears to be the number 53 on the turret side.

Oberstleutnant Hermann Balck from 2. Panzer-Division in his Befehlswagen with a second Befehlswagen behind. His tank appears to be an Ausf. G with extra armor over the driver and radio operator's front plate. Note the dummy main gun and dummy co-axial machine gun next to it. Both tanks are completed in overall Dunkelgrau, with the Balkenkreuz on the hull side. [Bundesarchiv]

A PzKpfw IV Ausf. D from 1. Zug, 6. Kompanie, II/3. Panzer-Regiment negotiating what looks to be a bridge constructed by one of their engineers. It is completed in overall Dunkelgrau, with its vehicle identification number 611 and a Balkankreuz on its hull side.

German infantry march past a PzKpfw III Ausf. G from I. Panzer-Regiment parked by the side of the road. It is completed in overall Dunkelgrau, with the divisional insignia to the right of the driver's visor. Above the driver's visor is the number 65432. It also appears to have a spade playing cards symbol on the turret. [Gregory Collection]

German troops inspect a PzKpfw III Ausf. G from 1 Zug, 5. Kompanie, II/3. Panzer-Regiment that appears to been set on fire after being hit by artillery. It is completed in overall Dunkelgrau, with its vehicle identification number 513 on the hull side.

Crews preparing to load a PzKpfw IV from 1. Zug, 3. Kompanie, I/3 Panzer-Regiment onto a freighter at Patras in May. It is completed in overall Dunkelgrau with its identification number 314 on the hull side.

PzKpfw III Ausf. Gs from 3. Panzer-Regiment part in a victory parade in Athens at the conclusion of the campaign. They are completed in overall Dunkelgrau and carry the divisional insignia to the right of the driver's visor. The tank on the right has a white rectangle on its turret and its identification number, 522, behind the Balkenkreuz on the hull. [Bundesarchiv]

5. Panzer-Division

A German recovery team working on the PzKpfw III Ausf. G from 31. Panzer-Regiment that was knocked out during the attack on Molos on 24 April. It is completed in overall Dunkelgrau. [Lee Archer]

This PzKpfw III Ausf. G tank from 31. Panzer-Regiment was knocked out during the attack on Molos on 24 April 1941 after it attempted to turn around and escape. It is completed in overall Dunkelgrau. [Lee Archer]

[This page] **This PzKpfw IV Ausf. B of 31. Panzer-Regiment was one of the ones knocked out at Molos on 24 April. It is completed in overall Dunkelgrau. [Lee Archer]**

This PzKpfw III Ausf. G tank from 31. Panzer-Regiment was also knocked out at Molos on 24 April 1941. It is completed in overall Dunkelgrau. [Lee Archer]

A 15 cm sIG33 (Sf) auf PzKpfw I Ausf. B from 5. Panzer-Division in Greece. It is completed in overall Dunkelgrau, with the unit insignia on the lower front plate above the number 704 and a Balkenkreuz on the superstructure side.

The crew of this Leichter Panzerspähwagen (MG) SdKfz 221 from 5. Panzer-Division have parked it below the Acropolis in Athens. It is completed in overall Dunkelgrau and carries the name "Houx" on the side plate, along with its Balkankreuz, the cross version of the divisional insignia. [Bundesarchiv]

The Schwerer Panzerspähwagen (Fu) SdKfz 232 8-rad (WH-230748) from 5. Panzer-Division in Athens. It is completed in overall Dunkelgrau and carries the name "Seydlitz" on the side plate. [Bundesarchiv]

191. Sturmgeschütz-Abteilung

[This page] StuG III Ausf. Bs from 191. Sturmgeschütz-Abteilung on their way through Katerini. All vehicles are completed in overall Dunkelgrau, with the Balkenkreuz on the superstructure side. [Bundesarchiv]

A StuG III Ausf. B from 191. Sturmgeschütz-Abteilung on its way to Athens. It is completed in overall Dunkelgrau, while on the side of the superstructure it has the Balkenkreuz and its unit insignia. Its unit insignia is also on the front left mudguard, while the tactical marking of an assault gun battery is on the left mudguard. [Gunther Geucke]

Other armor

A PzKpfw I Ausf. B passing an abandoned Guy-Ant Field Artillery Tractor in Greece. It is completed in overall Dunkelgrau. The meaning of its tactical symbol on its front plate is unclear.

A Kleiner Panzerfunkwagen (MG) SdKfz 260 in Greece. It is completed in overall Dunkelgrau and has a prominent Balkankreuz, painted over its engine radiator.

A PzKpfw IV on the road in Greece makes its way past captured British and Commonwealth prisoners of war. It is completed in overall Dunkelgrau and carries the Balkenkreuz on the turret rear. [Bundesarchiv]

[Below left] A PzKpfw III Ausf. F from 9. Panzer-Division on the road between Ptolemais and Kozani on 14 April. It is completed in overall Dunkelgrau, with its divisional marking on the left side of the front plate.

These two Schwerer Panzerspähwagen SdKfz 231 8-rad are most probably from Leibstandarte SS Adolf Hitler. Both vehicles are completed in overall Dunkelgrau, while the lead vehicle has the licence plate SS-1088. [Bundesarchiv]

Schützenpanzerwagen SdKfz 251/1s taking part in a victory parade in Athens. They are completed in overall Dunkelgrau, with the Balkankreuz on the hull side and rear. [NAC]

German armor on Crete

German plans for the invasion of Crete called for the landing of a small armored force at Kastelli Kissamou. This was to be drawn from the five PzKpfw IIs and 17 PzKpfw IIIs of 5. (Leicht) Kompanie of 31. Panzer-Regiment that had been left behind when 5. Panzer-Division pulled out of Greece. This was to be used to establish Panzer-Kompanie Kreta. First, however, the area had to be secured and this had been assigned to a small detachment of men under Leutnant Mürbe from one of the parachute battalions.

Almost from the start this went horribly wrong. Mürbe's detachment was intercepted by the Greek regiment in the area and local villagers and all but wiped out. The survivors took shelter in an old farmhouse until persuaded to surrender. Any plans to rescue them and bring the tanks over also had to be put on hold because of the tenuous situation of the main forces that had landed around Maleme airfield and Suda Bay. Even after the situation there had improved for the better by the withdrawal of New Zealand troops from the airfield there would be no respite for the survivors from Mürbe's force for several days because the situation around Maleme and Suda Bay was far from secure. This was compounded by the Royal Navy intercepting the seaborne invasion forces and sinking many of the craft, forcing the rest to return to Greece. Thus, it was not until 24 May 1941 that the German paratroopers launched an attack on Kastelli Kissamou and though the surviving paratroopers of Mürbe's detachment were rescued that day, it took three more days of heavy fighting before they were able to capture the harbour.

Thus, finally, on 28 May two PzKpfw IIs were towed across to Crete on a large wooden lighter by a small harbour tug. On reaching a suitable landing area the tug cast off the lighter and pushed it onto the beach. Explosive charges were then used to blow off the bow of the lighter and the tanks driven ashore. Unfortunately, the tanks arrived too late to have any real effect on the fighting, instead they were sent along the coast to join up with the mountain troops in the advance eastwards. Two days later, as part of the advanced guard of this force, they reached Rethymno and helped secure the surrender of the Australian and Greek troops there.

Generalmajor Richard Heidrich stops to talk to crews of one of the PzKpfw II Ausf. Cs landed on Crete in May. The tank is completed in overall Dunkelgrau. [Shaun Winkler]

One of the first two PzKpfw II Ausf. Cs landed on Crete in May 1941. It is completed in overall Dunkelgrau. [Shaun Winkler]

The Germans sent more tanks over to Crete after the battle, among them this PzKpfw 38(t), which by November 1943 had been dug in as a gun emplacement.

Color Plates

A Leichter Gepanzerter Beobachtungskraftwagen SdKfz 253, licence plate WH-685592, from 184. Sturmgeschütz-Abteilung in Yugoslavia in April 1941. It is completed in overall Dunkelgrau with a Balkenkreuz on both sides of the hull side. Its vehicle identification number, 31, appears in white on both sides and the hull rear. The yellow tactical symbol of an assault gun battery is on the front plate.

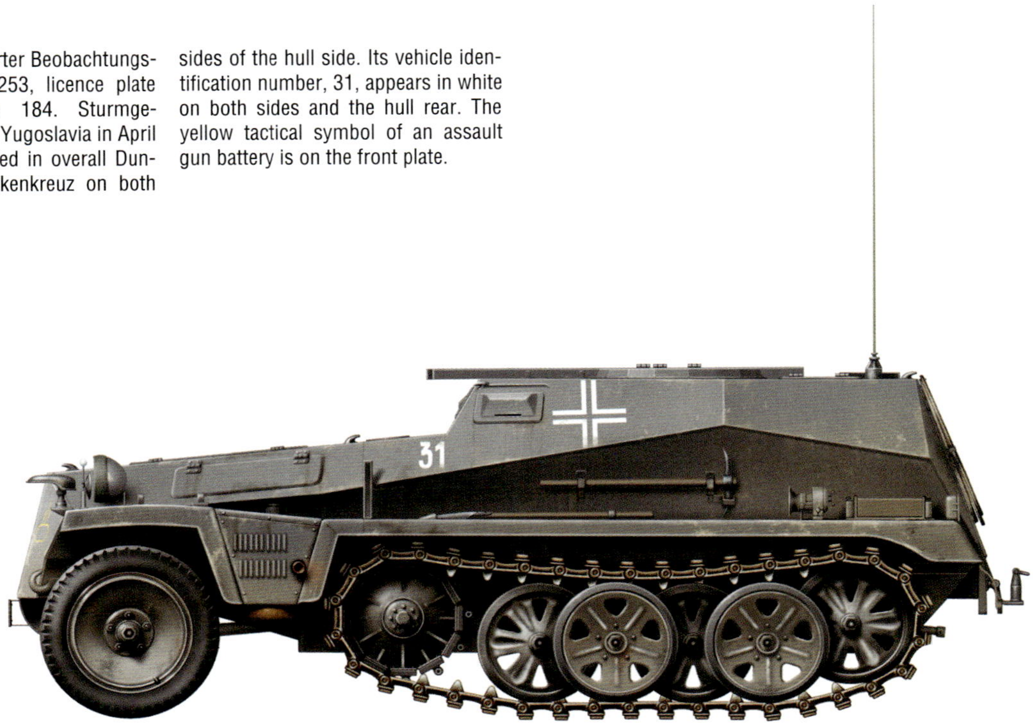

All color plates in this book (except the front cover) are reproduced to 1/35th scale

A Leichter Panzerspähwagen (MG) SdKfz 221 from 5. Panzer-Division in Athens in April 1941. It is completed in overall Dunkelgrau and carries the name "Houx" in white on the side plate, along with its Balkenkreuz. The cross version of the divisional insignia appears in yellow behind the Balkenkreuz and between the name and its yellow tactical symbol of a motorized recon company.

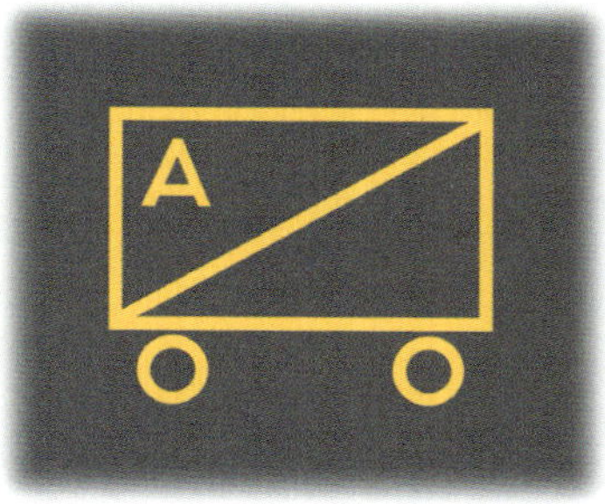

A Schwerer Panzerspähwagen (Fu) SdKfz 232 8-rad (WH-230748) from 5. Panzer-Division, as photographed in Lamia and later Athens in April 1941. It is completed in overall Dunkelgrau and carries the name "Seydlitz" in white on the side plate. It carries the divisional sign of 5. Panzer-Division in white in front of its name.

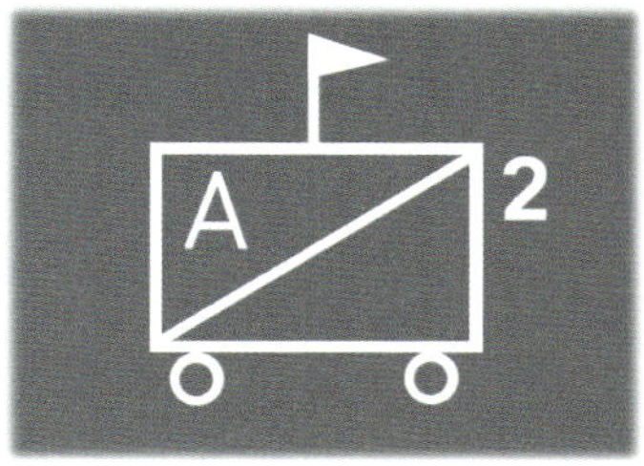

Below & bottom left A Sturmgeschütz III Ausf. B from 184. Sturmgeschütz-Abteilung in Yugoslavia in April 1941. It is completed in overall Dunkelgrau and carries on the side of the superstructure the Balkenkreuz, along with its white vehicle identification number, 34. It also carries the Balkenkreuz on the roof of the superstructure.

A PzKpfw III Ausf. F (manufactured by M.A.N. Werk Nuernberg), from I/3. Panzer-Regiment, 2. Panzer-Division near Platamon on 17 April 1941. It is completed in overall Dunkelgrau, while it carries on its side plate in yellow the divisional insignia (above which is the chassis number 61016). Next to it are in white the tactical symbol of tank company with number beside it, a Balkenkreuz and its identification number 123. On the turret it carries a spade playing card symbol.

Below left & below A Sturmgeschütz III Ausf. B from 191. Sturmgeschütz-Abteilung near Athens in April 1941. It is completed in overall Dunkelgrau, while on the side of the superstructure it has the Balkenkreuz and the unit insignia of a red bull in a black rectangle outlined in red. Its unit insignia is also on the front right mudguard, while the tactical marking of an assault gun battery is on the front left mudguard.

A PzKpfw IV Ausf. E from 15. Panzer-Regiment, 11. Panzer-Division in Yugoslavia in April 1941. The tank is completed in overall Dunkelgrau, with the yellow divisional insignia in between driver's visor and the hull machine gun mount. The divisional insignia also appears in front of the driver's side visor, followed by the division's ghost insignia, further back beside the Balkenkreuz on the hull side. It also carries a vehicle identification number 11 below the visor on the turret side.

Below & below right A PzKpfw II Ausf. B or C from 14. Panzer-Division in Zagreb on 11 April 1941. It is completed in overall Dunkelgrau, with the divisional insignia in yellow to the right side of the driver's visor. It has a Balkenkreuz on the hull side and a yellow vehicle identification of IL2 on the turret side. The yellow dot behind the vehicle number on the turret was the sign of 36. Panzer-Regiment when it was part of 4. Panzer-Division and was retained by the regiment when it became part of 14. Panzer-Division.

Below & bottom right First Lieutenant Galli's M13/40 (R^{o}E^{TO} 2815) from 4th Medium Tank Battalion, 131 Divisione Corazzato "Centauro" that was knocked out at Monastir Hill, March 1941. It is completed in overall Italian dark grey-green (Grigoverde), with three vertical stripes in a red rectangle indicating it was from the 3rd Platoon of the 1st Company. The letter IV below it meaning it was from the 4th Medium Tank Battalion. This marking is repeated on the rear hull plate. The playing card insignia of seven diamonds on a rectangle was a platoon identification marking used only in the Balkans. The white circle on the turret is an air recognition symbol.

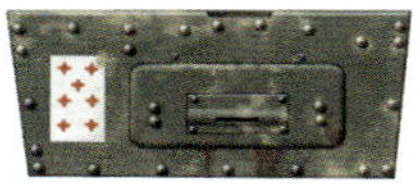

A 38M Toldi I light tank (H-322) of 1 Felderítő Zászlóalj (1st Reconnaissance Battalion) in Reghin during the Hungarian occupation of northern Transylvania in September 1940. It is completed in a three-tone scheme of dark olive green, oversprayed with bands of ochre and red-brown. On the turret sides behind the hatches and glacis plate it has the Maltese-style Hungarian cross of a white cross outlined with red and a green circle around the boss. Forward of the cross on the turret is the official emblem of the Motorized Branch, which includes the Hungarian National crest. This was applied as a transfer to the vehicle. Its registration number, H-322, is inside a white rectangle. In between the letter H and the number is the red/white/green Hungarian shield. It has the white lightning bolt of the unit insignia on the right front and right rear mudguard.